SUMMER SKIES

MAHIBAH AHMED

Made with ♥ on the Notion Press Platform
www.notionpress.com

To dreamers

Contents

Contents

Contents

Contents

Preface

This book is written over the sunlit May, a lackadaisical June, a warm July, and a somewhat nostalgic August of 2023.

While a golden filter was cast upon everything and sunflowers were tucked neatly in a corner and as the small window in my room flooded it with sunlight, I wrote these lines.

Summer brings me happiness, loads of it. But it also brings out a sadness in me.

When the sky is a bit too blue and you hate it, not because it's blue but because it might never be that blue again.

When the sun is shining through every crack yet you feel empty because there's part of your soul cursed with eternal clouds that no sunlight can reach.

But more than everything, it brings happiness. The shapes in the clouds, the fields of flowers; sunrays painting everything golden and simple joys.

The little things, great memories, songs on guitar, bicycle rides, and the shades of the summer skies at sunsets.

You think about it in the moment and you think about it again when you find dry flowers pressed in the pages of a book.

Warmth.

Nostalgia.

Joy.

Solitude.

Introduction

23rd March 2024

"When we look up at the sky, we are not only gazing into the great depths of the unknown but maybe also a piece of us that we can't quite see on the ground. Some thoughts refuse to settle and float in the air, and hence, when we look into that vast mirror, we can finally reflect upon and catch those in our eyes."

5th June 2023

"The sound of the rain taps on my soul and evokes in me the miseries I have locked away. A sense of history, unacknowledged wounds, and taint on the glory that the rain fails to wash away, years upon years."

20th June 2023

"Summer is carried in us in the little fragments of the joys that we steal from paper planes and summer vacations, and clouds sailing across the sky. The sunsets, the memories, the blessing that is sunshine generously poured into your existence and life comes easily to you."

3rd July 2023

"The sight of the skies leads me into daydreams, the thoughts and fantasies I thought I could not touch from the ground. It lifts you in its hazy demeanor and leads you into the places and the stories that are far too magnificent to exist and yet, as a dreamer, you had the privilege."

29th July 2023

"Sometimes the sunrays fail to light up the dark that consumes us. It drowns us in its undercurrent. When the sky is a bit too blue for your liking and the crowds are a bit too happy but you are empty, alone, and tired. You have felt that, maybe, and I have too."

7th August 2023

"The quiet anxiety that sets your soul ricocheting between what you have done and what you are to do, what you should have done and what you could now do as you watch the sun fade into a distant glimmer. Existential crises crash like waves upon the shore that is your peace of mind and leave permanent scars of salt and ravines upon ravines and you fear that you were much better before and you will never be as good again."

25th August 2023

"The summer air wields the power to revive the memories in you with the shade of the sky or that shell that you found out of nowhere and the urge to retrace your paths and reopen the now-rusted doors of your past. Some sweet, some bitter, some better-forgotten memories that the sunrays spark back into the fire that they were. Nostalgia. Emptiness in you where those memories once were. The thought that maybe that was the last time you felt something and you just attained the age to realize it."

amber skies.

1. never really

crumbled it in my hand
i never really cared
fumbled to take my stand
justice wasn't fair
afraid to hold a hand
love was never in the air
stared at the depth but backed
i never really dared
i looked death in the eyes
when i couldn't stand this air
thought i almost seized the prize
but i was never really there
when the pain tried to numb me
my heart had known more tears
when i wanted the seven seas
i never really fared
when the shades of sky ran with me
my thoughts were lost somewhere
when the moon and sun were done with me
i never really stared
and then one day i let me go
and let the free winds steer
i stood with friends i dared the foe

hesitant, yes, but never really scared.

2. mirror

if you get home everyday
and fall upon the bed
and don't need a mirror to reflect
if you say things you don't mean
and then you regret
and try to patch them up in your head
if you have the pride of a queen
that you think you are
and hate to say what's on your mind
if it's a bit too hard to keep it all inside
you're much too honest to be considered kind
so you distance yourself a bit too far
if you feel the way you feel
and you don't deny
and don't deserve this walk with head low
if you hate to raise your broken voice
but you say it anyway so you made a lot of foes
so you soak up all the tears you cry
if you can dare to gaze each day
in a broken mirror on the wall
with a broken reflection of broken you
and be brave enough to own yourself
take it as another day in life to do

and hold your head high in an empty hall
if you can manage to find in the reflection
another better you gazing right through
the cracks and flaws of yourself you hide
you just need sunlight from within your eyes
and you shall again rise like full moon tides
and accept the weird mess you call "you"

if you can hold together your broken pieces
and try to make something and make it
that you can forever be proud of
a scream of colour, out of a prism
out of a grey gently weeping cloud
you don't fake it, darling, you make it
you are a mess of mirrors that lead the way
you are your own moon, night and day
you have the courage and what it takes
you are a mirror at night, rainbow by day.

3. the side of me that i conceal

no i have truly never known myself
or owned for that matter, what i call me
no i have never grown into this skin
and the quill is the only mirror i see me in
when the simplistic pleasures are few
and i arise good as new
but then there is a side of me that i
i feel but know enough of pride to conceal
a side of this flower tends to let go
a side of it tends to hold on and so
there's a side of it that smile with tears in eyes
and a side that just simply breaks and cries
a side of me that faces the sun and
a side that lurks in shadows that run
a heart that is fragile yet hard to break
a laugh that is agile and hard to fake
within me lives a soul that wants to fly up to the stars
and shares the space with another one
that is just bleeding with all the scars
two minds in me, one deals with the world and stays low
the other one flies to a world they'll never know
half of my heart loves you to moon and back

but the other half just watched you go
i can't hide my joy but my sadness i conceal
i will never know of love but that's what i feel
words in my head too sharp to speak
within me the two roads an agreement seek
who knows with whom destiny struck a deal
am i all that i truly feel or all i do conceal?

4. art

the deep skies within your eyes
the lie you buried did not die
the brokenness in the fragile heart
caused by someone's sin, turned into art
shatter my thoughts before i even string them
what once mattered is now a godforsaken gem
i gave something that never existed my all
now i try to catch my tears before they fall
i wasn't a masterpiece that i always tried to be
i was broken deeper than the eyes could see
catching breezes that were never there
patching up my dreams that no one shared
there existed yet more ways to shine than be a gem
it's all still yours no matter how greatly it's broken
instead of falling in coal mine after absorbing the pain
like pieces of a mosaic i put myself together again.

5. i am sorry i forget

i am sorry i forget to apologise
for things i did, it takes some tries
to find out your real self in the thick crowd
of all these hearts of stones you build about
all these versions of yourself you confine
in this little soul, balancing on tightrope lines
and all these people you don't want to let down
all the while struggling to cease your crown
so i apologise if i ever made you frown

i am sorry i forget, i forget to realise
that my coldness hurts, it takes some tries
to find right people, to make new friends
to forget the past and begin new ends
for living in the past does you no good
relive memories, trail paths to where you stood
and all these people holding me tight
maybe that web is why i can't see the light
so i apologise for losing trust, falling from heights

i am sorry, i forget to tell this to you
if i ever in losing me i lost you too
you had a dream upon that summer, i made it wilt

i left you there unapologetic, but i still feel the guilt
i didn't mean to i swear but when the fog lifts
i dare not look me in the eyes as sands of time sift
again in the dread of darkness, i wander these halls
dreaming of old days and upon me the moonlight falls
i can't forgive me either let alone you, for missing calls

i am sorry i forget, to admit that i too feel
i am a human and i err because i'm real
all the hustling in big cities and losing in maps
too busy to look up and stitch up all the gaps
that i couldn't fill in because i didn't know me
but here as it rains i realise it is meant to be
regretful if i don't let it go, painful if i let the story sew
so once again i am sorry, i forget to tell you
that i am a human and i deserve some apologies too.

6. where the sun sets in a different hue

when at the sight of a sunset i held my breath

as the shades of the sky faded and changed

as the sun emerged and then in grace it set

from bright to sombre hues it ranged

and i headed east in search of memories

in search of the shades i long hadn't seen

and then as if the time since had seized

i found them exactly where they had been

i headed west for inspiration and dreams

that i had never before witnessed in my time

i had known it to spark colours that screamed

i ventured and the legends hold it true as defined

i headed north to seek the truth if it ever was

to find the sunsets an everlasting glimmer

and there i found the sun rays on the ice's flaws

and as the dusk progressed, it faded to a shimmer

i headed south as the moon chased the sun

the sky was settling in a different hue

and i saw the sun and the moon on the run

the stars light the path they choose

and then i came back, homesickness is a pain

the places i haven't seen, i have not a clue

the places that aren't marked on maps, hence fare again
to where the sun sets in a different hue.

7. forget-me-not

summer air asking me to care
about each moment, each memory, each run
now long into time we have fared
embodied what we thought we'd never become
but you sent me forget-me-nots
fearing i would forget it all
can i bear to forget few of the lots
that turn my summers into falls?
the same memories that brightened my dreams
now end up in nightmare screams
the way all the sweet flowers rot
and yet their sweet memory mocks
the way all the rotten flowers are forgotten
you were hardest of all being a forget me not
we blame each other and blame the wrong
when it was our fault all along
gentle rain darkens the day
no knowledge of ahead what lay
wildflowers don't give up this soon
should i send some forget-me-nots too?
it will be gone, it will be lost
and the summer clouds turn into frosts
these flowers will perish, the memory linger

of love there are no true harbingers

here's a solemn vow and here's an applause

i won't forget you, and clever choice of flower pots

so just as much pain it may cause

as a faithful friend and foe, forget me not.

8. komorebi

the light was breaking through the canopies

"it's komorebi" she said to me

under the patches of shadows and lights

it was a mesmerizing sight

and she poured in some tea

the cherry blossoms were in the air

it was deep silence; it was rare

the sun dawned upon my life

the tokyo streets came alive

i thought of the dream that got me here

the shops, the temples and bullet trains

through the canopies the dew drops rained

an element of rush hangs in the air

while in my leisure i observe with care

i reflected on this being one of life's many lanes

then the morning warmed my soul

empty inside, my heart felt whole

komorebi echoed and to this day it echoes

i will fade but these canopies will quote

the light broke through the cracks in my soul

like komorebi, and my heart felt whole.

9. thoughts when i look in the mirror

why do i look this this.
could have been much better
like my hair could have been less frizzy
and my eyes always look dizzy
never mind.
i hate my reflection, if it was water i'd stir it
if it was a broken word, i'd slur it
yet i'd keep it as how i know myself
the mirror is only where we meet ourselves.
i guess.
does the world run on perfect hair?
or by angels, fairies and diamonds rare?
maybe "pretty" is just a word in the dictionary
some standards have to be met
maybe not.
pretty really is just a word
not all standards are to be matched by you
not all boxes to be ticked by you
if you can own your hair and you skin and everything about
you
so please
dear, if you can do all that why hear the few

that will go on with their words that will cut like knife
but remember this, beyond all that lies a bigger life
a bigger place, with larger dreams and greater promises
why ever worry your mind?
there are more things to learn that to regret
there are more things than to look in a mirror and curse
yourself
so please can you for once not be so rough
on all your scars and marks that you want to get rid of
we all are unique so stop comparing.
because a human is their heart and soul and mind
you should not care if in this cruel world you're still kind
you can light up streets with power in your walk
you can break all their standards and shut them when they
talk
believe me.
you're going to be alright
there's really no right or wrong size
we were all just meant to end up like humans that we are
if you have some, then celebrate the fact you have scars
tell me.
why can't you see? does the mirror make you blind?
there's more wisdom and strength inside of you than you can
confine
yes, it's hard to be perfect, who'd know better than me
but what's harder is owning yourself and building a
personality

so why not take a step back

love yourself

and say

"i will prove them all wrong today".

rainy days.

10. dial tone

i am sitting on my bed
a half covered window that lets sunlight in
busy brooklyn under my wings
some sadness over me swims
in front of the overly decorated walls
in the sober joy of solitude
my guitar sits there
killing time, i am on the phone
the dial tone reminds me of
all the 80s songs the wood has known
and the promises i didn't keep
you realise it too late to weep
the dial tone goes on
in the eerie silence of the day
a foreboding of doom hangs in the air
the dial tone rings on
reminds me of some billy joel song
too heavy of a grief to dance with today
the anxiety, the way a slow moment speeds up for you
yet stays the same for everything around you
the tension rises, what if-
"no more thoughts!" i tell myself
it is picked up now!

"she is no more"
i drop the phone
my guitar still sits there killing time
the sun still shines
everything is the same in this room
deep down and for me it's all upside down
there's no joy in being alone
i wish the dial tone never ended.

11. origami crane

beside the bed of a child
a basket is laid
as the war is going outside
blood is paid
a disease not known
till distant times
no apologies, no forgiveness
for unacknowledged crimes
the blood is drained, a slow death
the barely breathing child coughs
the parting is clear but unsaid
death comes easy when time are rough
a piece of paper shows no hope
yet she tries to fold one
it wilts, she tries her best to cope
the sweating hands, boiling sun
the child coughs, gunfire rages
the remedies failed, no one left to cry
the burning days remembered for ages
there were no tears left to dry
beside the bed was a basket laid
the last crane still in her hand
for the wars, innocence was paid

a breeze set the crane to land
as still as may and quiet as june
there was silence then
not a hope, not a siren, not a tune
wars of women, wars of men
beside the bed a basket was leaned
a thousand but one less
that was the crane that should have been
the key to set free from illness
that was the time, the desperate age
when hope was rare, down bloody lanes
when too much blood stained the page
people put their faith in paper cranes.

12. rainy cab ride

drops eased down the pane
immortal grieves down the lane
clouds set dull and sky did grey
this fistful of melancholy i called a day
like pearls they collected on the cold window
till they dripped down like tears and settled low
this rage of thought but absence of words
amidst the mist and sights that are blurred
questions that will never find a voice
to hold the tongue is the only choice
i search for my speech, raindrops run like nile
i am known to draw silences that out length miles
an emptiness still hangs in the air between
two foes that were friends in a long lost dream
and to speak is to risk, to keep silence is sore
you and i ended right here like an old folklore
i dare say my hopes did end in vain
no, i did not feel the rain
the way i always do but today
today it felt like a different day
the rain on my side, sun on another
the way you and i ignore each other
this silence is killing me inside

just as much as this rainy cab ride.

13. come home

you have trodden all paths that run
you have seen different skies and suns
lived in tokyo, travelled all rome
does your heart still live at home?
skyscrapers, hustling, unknown faces
in the middle of crowds is the loneliest place
big friends and bigger foes you've found
would you still come homeward bound?
the city of dreams and city of love
do they all compare to stars above
seen from rooftop on a clear night
or are you used to unhomely heights?
all the hues the sun could set in
running from cities, can't run from sins
fare these oceans, lose in the maps
does the home in your heart stitch the gap?
home is where the heart is, free to roam
but did your heart ever leave this home?
in denial, but you still think of oak trees
are they all formed as homely epiphanies?
you have chased fame, name under lights that blind
what you're looking for is what you left behind
you have lost the old for what was new

does homesickness ever get the better of you?
your eyes don't shine like the stars they were
have you lost the meaning you were searching for?
how great the distances i have not a clue
just know, the stars back home miss you too
just know that there will be unknown places
so long as you shall roam
but if you ever miss familiar faces
you can always come home.

14. secret to surviving

we have played with silence long enough
it hasn't really made a difference
i believed summer for the good was tough
never expected this suffering
i'm gasping for air, finding my breath
finding the soul i locked in my heart
trust is fragile, it dies an easy death
yet it takes a while to build a part
keeping my head up in the clouds
the grief beneath suffocates the air
escapism is foolish, i accept it loud
resorting to it is last thing i swear
i would have held on to the last shred
what i wouldn't pay time to rewind
sell all i love, take back what i said
hold the string when they could no more grind
they say that life is not more than a lie
my belief in that is ever stronger
but after all the cuts that time brought by
i am trying to live this lie a little longer
when all you had is lost, life feels like a lie
you forget to breathe, wishing you could die
just remember to hold on a little longer

it might just be alright; you just have survived.

15. hourglass

time fixes everything, just wait
just watch the sands run
life comes full circle they say
after many moons, many suns
led me to question this eternal promise
universe exists because of uncertainty so
to test the patience of a curse or bliss
i knocked the hourglass, teased time, my foe
to my shattered heart, i could not bring
content, as it lay in time that had passed
if time can fix just everything
will it fix a broken hourglass?
it does not reverse it, sands bury the crime
nothing has ever or will stay as it was
it never fixes but numbs and takes time
you only learn to live with broken glass.

16. grey is the colour of falling apart

it all started one stupid spring
i didn't think it would stick through
but it defied me and did the worst it could do
spring ended and heat waves lashed
in summer i feared it would be worse
and it did, our hopes abashed
wisdom was sour, stuck in a curse
and the holidays went down in grief
in autumn we saw some hope
it was better, under falling leaves
then i was told i need to cope
damn this long known fragility of peace
autumn then gracefully fell into winter
a broken heart a solution seeks
i wish they would fall again in winter
then it all blossomed into spring again
it was broken for good, i cried, i should
i realised inevitable was the pain
my heart was swollen as sea with regret
i tried to get drunk on my epiphanies
when we'd all be together but i forget
when reality is no good, fancies are the keys

the year went too fast, too swiftly
things went rough rather quickly
i tried hard but the game was rigged
the hands let go of hold, destiny tricked
and outside the courtroom i sat there crying
between two fates that never intertwined
they cried buckets too but inside
and the rest were screaming inside with joy
"there ends their joy, good people wrong choice"
it was my fault, i could have fixed it
had i worked harder on them than i did
and walked out of the court with eyes
filled with tears too much to see the sky
and the sky, it was all shades of lies
i stood there and they opened their cars
saw the sunset sky, smiled or cried, fell apart
but held their heart and went their own ways
the sky, it was that spring, that night, that day
but for my tear-drenched eyes, it was just grey.

17. dandelion

i put faith in a dandelion
and i don't know when it's seeds all blew
if that was an expression of true faith
or just a coincidence
one of a few
so there are little things that i believe in
so call it my devoted faith if you may
but when you put faith in dandelions
even little things make your day.

18. tears will fall to futility

what worth are tears, they fall down anyway
and dry up and leave no trace
what worth is this smile you fake all day
and fall on the bed and retrace
every step you took that led you here
regret not speaking when you could
but it wasn't at all your fault dear
the world is not running as it should
they don't tell you this but you realise
you can't feel everything they hit your way
you can't shed all the tears in your eyes
sometimes you learn to hold tears through the day
futile tears, they have grown up with years
but the world will learn civility
but even then the truth will be, i fear
that the tears will fall to futility.

Sunshine.

19. june flowers

it always gets to me no matter how hard i try
when my thoughts like a rain cloud ease
upon my deep-set eyes
when my heavy soul in shallow showers drown
in the early hours of summer eves
as rain comes pouring down
those clouds do live inside my eyes
and are the reason for daydreams
but the sight of wet roses suffices
midsummer is now about to burst in rains
in a shaded wet tropical and it seems that
the lily dances, the hydrangea faints
my dahlias fell in bloom and grieves put to dust
the hibiscus soon wilted, lavenders dwelled
i remember all rains, i must
and among the falling raindrops i fathom a tune
rare of me to make music so well
of flowers i grew in june.

20. paper planes

scribbled words upon a page

never attain the dignity of age

crumble in the child's hand

soaring dreams before they land

floating on the sunlit air

catching breezes that were never there

upon a summer afternoon

when you can see the sun, run the moon

the little pages must wilt and turn

these summer nostalgic stories and guilt will burn

warm memories pressed within

the creases of a page, racing in the air to win

chasing winds, soaring heights

flying in the summer winds under the sun light

like a bird that knows the air it flies

faster than the fastest spreading wildfire lies

a touch of innocence, a shade of light

in the words that now flew out of sight

the worst is when you know it will never come back

but it will one day, out of the many memories in the stack

then the plane can no more be seen

it has flown away in the wind, it has long been

the paper planes will fly and soar, rough and mild

till it falls in the hand of another child.

21. sea breeze

through a half-open window
a summer-y breeze finds it's way
in a sunlit hall darkened by my shadow
where stringing blank verses i stay
it flipped some pages, trapped the words
shook off the dreams in the dreamcatcher
a sense of summer in me felt absurd
as in my soul it struck a match
lighting the ocean i could see clear
all in my head but it all felt a bit real
all i felt was what was not here
the glistening sea in shades of teal
a taste of salt, a glimmer of sea
the wind from the ocean blows differently
leading sailors to where they ought to be
yet it led my mind to this epiphany.

22. bonfire in june

the dusk was dawning in the air
we struck matches and lit a fire
with summer flowers stuck in my hair
living was a need, a need much dire
the fire grew, memories made
the tides in the sea ebbed and swelled
the air around held the sparks in the shade
our memories around the fire dwelled
this was the first and the last we'd feel this
the best or worst in our times
we have all we need yet we miss
what is long gone in distant times
we sing of glory, we speak of joy
we remember the memories we made by
through the life's streams a sailor's voyage
all the worst we have seen and we did not die
so here is a night to celebrate
the people, the cheer of the past years
when we felt and accepted our fates
but it changed over time, drowned in our tears
so here's to the old that we went through
here's to the tingle of the new tune
we dared to dream told our stories that were true

around a bonfire upon a midnight in june.

23. polaroid

in the sunflower fields upon a long-lost may

when the air was warm, i had nothing left to say

a hat on my head that hid my dark eyes

summer is foolish for the young, for the old it's wise

i am not here to regret today, i am here to face the sun

and feel the sunshine on my face, seek the shadows that run

as if the dust of gold by some fairy was left on the flowers

but it was only sunlight and my golden fancy's dreamiest hour

i always had a belief in my soul that summer carries dreams

now for the first time i know it is bestowed on us as sunbeams

easy winds now gently lift the soul that had gone down

in the coldest feelings of that march, all it wore was a frown

but here the light of the day shines bright on me

and i accepted this as my fate that was meant to be

i was never a winter that i always thought of me

i was a summer in the yellowest of sunflower field

ribbon in my hair, sunflower air dizzies my long-wearied head

makes me spin around in a whirl of warm words that you said

it was the colours, the warmth, your joy and my soul's serenity

and you captured it in a piece of paper and framed it for

eternity.

24. from the tea table on a rainy day

gently boiling as the summer storm lashes

and takes out all the light away

so you light a candle that gives gentle ashes

a gentle flame rises on a rough day

through the kitchen window

as the tea ebbs and swells and simmers

like the storm outside that goes

leaves the glass in a mesmerizing glimmer

gently pour and strain your share

and feel the gush of the steam

that erupts from the chinaware

as if a mist covering you in a dream

who knew fragile chinaware holds some ease

sugar cubes, be generous

don't count anything else but memories

a little sweetness won't hurt

the peace is settling in the atmosphere

i dare not ruin it with a song

the feeling of warming chill is almost rare

being alone and loneliness were different all along

so cherish a moment of solitary existence

a luxury that to few is known

and sink into the rhythm of rain that dances
with your thoughts when you're alone
then all at once it is not there
you stir up a piece of that fantasy
you have never truly known life dear
if it was raining and you didn't make tea.

25. take a break

how have you been lately
i haven't been able to ask
do you still remember how the world looks
when you look up from your tasks?
so i'd take this moment to ask you
how have you really been
or you're simply existing
and avoiding being seen
so how long has it been...
since you heard your favourite songs
and threw your hands up in the air
let it go and carried along?
since when have you been so dull
back in high school you were the star
lighting everywhere you went
now we barely even see where you are
how long has it really been…
since you blocked out all the chatters
and did not let your anxiety cave in
and held yourself as what mattered
you never even think of you anymore
do you ever sit alone at afternoon tea
and think about all you have

and not all that you could have been
so take this as a warning to rest your head
and look in retrospect how far you have run
you have done the best you could have done
so pour yourself some love tonight
and just take a break, hun.

26. life goes on

life goes on
through the mountains, through the lanes
through the rivers and their plains
and as rough or tender life may seem
a slender chance to exist it has been
so life goes on
like a cloud that sails
yes it goes on like the ice that hails
and it flows like the currents in rivers and gleams
life has not been all that it has seemed
and life went on
and led me to different roads
with happiness in hand and grief in the load
and smooth sailing it can't be labelled
yet every time i stumbled i have been stabled
and this is what we call life
i have known this winding road
you carry joys and grieves in your load
for forever as the road goes on and on
till they are forgotten enough to be gone
and life moves on
like the rows of tulips in dutch fields
like all the flowers that a plant can yield

and once again i stand and stare
how far i have come and i was unaware
and life? well, it is a long path
and being one on it i tread my miles
i catch my tears and put up smiles
it runs like blood and out lengths the nile
i am glad that it's been a while
life went on
too fast for me to catch its hold
i have lived, people spend their' s hoarding gold
the oceans and lands and seas i have fared
it has progressed, i have sat and stared
so life goes on
like the windmills on a windy day
like the tulip fields a bloom in may
into my existence it poured thunder and rains
healed my bruises and unacknowledged pains
and with life i went on too
through town streets and city lights
through sunlit dreams and blurred sights
and every breath you take in and let go
time passes fast so take it slow
and life will go on
one day you will sit and think
how all those years flashed in a blink
through all the needles in roads i have kneeled
but here i am in this tulip field

life goes on as it will but right now, it is still.

27. i have wished

i have wished upon dandelions and summer flowers
i have wished upon the near and distant stars
i have wished upon every clover i found
and i have crossed my fingers when i was bound
i have wished on winters, waited on springs
i have wished upon all the raindrops monsoon brings
i have wished upon all that has come and gone
i have wished upon scars i have long donned
i have wished upon the lands and seas
i have wished upon the ocean breeze
i have tried and had faith enough and dear
i have wished upon all that i found near
i have blessed, i have cursed, i have wished to change
my agonies from simple to worst pains have ranged
and here i stand, still faithful with all the scars
having hope enough to still wish on shooting stars.

28. goodbye, june!

the bougainvillea were bursting

it was spring and you were riding your cycle

faster than you could wink

and some unknown road was taken by you

to the train station

the air was golden and the wind was warm

the day was left gentle due to yesterday's storm

and some old memory from some old place

dragged you now and changed your pace

as you headed to the train station

unsaid words in your head as they spin

you controlled all your fancies and whims

to head back and run and hide and cry

you hadn't planned much, but you could still say bye

if you reached the station

faster in the name of unspoken confessions

slowed down by unacknowledged obsessions

but you went on and ignoring the beautiful day

the summer warmth and the flowers of may

because you were going to the train station

you flip the break and leave your bicycle

the train is about to leave, you have to hurry up

and you can't meet but still catch a glimpse

of something you knew but no more loved

standing at a platform

a tsunami of words tries to blurt out of your mouth

but all they hear is silence and indistinct chatter

your hand on the cold window and you see what you came for

the train was leaving, it was noisy, nothing you said would matter

on that train station

the train left and smiled at yourself and cried a bit too

sometimes you don't see what happiness is

till it is all taken away from you

but you pride yourself that you said some of what you came to say

just a small "goodbye, june!" with tears and a smile

as she would go apart now, miles upon miles

it's none of my business yet runs in my mind

heart is just indecisive, thoughts are hard to find

words don't come out the way you want sometimes

we don't beg for forgiveness on unacknowledged crimes

sometimes essays are misunderstood

but "goodbye, june" works just fine.

purple pink skies.

29. clouds

half-remembered numbers
faded in deep slumbers
heavy breaths and better
torn apart old letter
memory of grandmother
tales without a stutter
float in like air above me
sinking dreamy epiphanies
a softer form my fancies took
when at the open skies i looked.

30. july air

i stand on the sloping roof
of my ancestral house aloof
to feel the july air upon my face
taking breaths at a slower pace
remembering it wasn't all this way
the winds in july have less to say
the carpets stained with old story
the walls plagued with gold glory
a gush of warm air on my skin
memory of virtue, memory of sin
memory of time that i passed like this
looking at the sky, a heavenly bliss
under a bright sun where the sun rays kiss
the taste of sea salt in the floating air
the touch of faraway mists without a care
the monsoon damp upon my clothes
under my feet, ash of burning oaths
one afternoon i heard those spirits talk
they sailed on seas, on winds they walked
they buried the words they meant for me
but then july air burned them all free
it's funny to know how an airy breeze
can many an old memories ease

that was when i realised that there
july air is made of more than air.

31. airplane thoughts

i looked upon a sea of clouds
still as summer, not a sound
the sun was shining and i
i never blinked an eye
for in the sunrays i saw dreams
in the silence i heard the screams
the sunflowers were in the air
when the rest of the sky was blue and bare
lost in thoughts that i never fathomed
lost in what never will and what may come
lost in epiphanies lost in regrets
lost in flying as high as it gets
no my head isn't in the cloud today
no i'm not trying to fathom simple rain
i said i didn't care wherever i go
i said i would take life a little slow
and here i am on one of many life's roads
among the clouds my dreams found abode
breaking away i thought this true
the cage in my mind is still painted blue
i said i wanted to sail and i didn't care
fifty thousand feet up in the air
miles and miles up into the blue

here i am still thinking of you.

32. i felt the moon running away

i looked up into the sky
the storm had left in a darker shade
the moon was there and i
i stood and held my empty gaze
the storm had left and left it all
in a mess of greens and blues
the trees that once had stood tall
were now the ghost of it in a darker hue
but then i saw the moon try to run
the only hope that shone that night
till the dawn came with the sun
was the cold and seamless moonlight
the weather was hard and rough
the wind was a chilled
the tides were in crests and troughs
the sun had set on the distant hill
i had felt the moon running away
where the moon leaves, the dark shrouds
i crossed my fingers and wished upon the day
but i realised it was only the clouds.

33. some journeys end where they begin

in circles and stars around the moon

the way we dance before spirits fall too soon

all the freckles on my face, the sun, and my

life and luck since i opened my eyes

in the dreams and fancies under the rain

the infinite strains and the never-ending pains

the things too big for me to comprehend

all things do, and all must come to an end

long gazes into the dark and infinite wonders

if tomorrow will come easy or with thunders

when we have hope enough to rest our heads

and put the weariest of thoughts to bed

when a flower blooms and then it dries

when the winds blow in the eastern skies

they all come back to whence they came

the same things are disguised in different names

hence all that goes around comes around

the deeds always come homeward bound

hence look back as much as you look ahead as you run

some journeys only end where they once begun.

34. pixies in the meadows

i once found a fairy tale for me
and decided to live there for an eternity
i am known to have a wild fantasy
but then, daydreams got the better of me
i heard a tune in my head and weaved stories
and drifted to a place i had never known
and it was a path of memories and that of glories
through a garden where my dreams were sown
escaped the reality whenever i dreaded it
fix my life in my head when i couldn't say what i mean
dig up my regrets from where they embedded it
and undo them in my head as it should have been
reality is the hardest role i have to play i feel
i was always here and will always be as i know
it's childish to daydream so silence seals the deal
off to where fear doesn't exist, pixies tell tales in meadows
i run a justice system in my head and i
make rulings over things i can't control
i always sleep with one eye open at night
to watch my unreal but perfect life unfold
so cruel is the world that i have created in dreams
you can feel them more than anything else
yet intangible and forsaken by the reality it seems

touch nothing but have been through heavens and hells
it makes me feel more than my numb life, a potion in a vial
break away from the life i have been long enlisted
and yet here i am all alone and stuttering in denial
that how all i have ever loved and felt never even existed.

35. the taj

if you ever like me had *the* luck to visit

the greatest and the most prosperous of lands

saw the royal halls and had privilege to walked through it

mesmerized in all the polish the universe ever had

if only most had luck half as much as me

they would have known the feel of true royalty

if only they had the luck to see what i had seen

captured the moment as if she was walking out of a dream

she wears a crown on her head and a *taj* it's called

sits on the throne that is all her own in her own halls

walks in grace through the memory in the corridors

she is numb to her past but she remembers the folklores

she has lived through life and lived through *war*

she wears the greatest glory and knows what for

she wears a crown and it is fondly called a taj

and in the sunlit air she seems as true as a mirage

and all that comes out of her quill is a blur

to tell the truth i wish i could write like her

i feel in her she carries a part of me, i carry her's

if you speak in front of this majesty, all you utter is slur

she wears a crown on her head and a taj it's named

her velvet cloak swept the floor along as she came

embellished in rubies and sapphires the colour of her eyes

if the world is tainted with disgrace, this was the sweetest lie
she wears a taj and can hold her head up high against day
to the extent that women envy her gold but the men fall prey
and her footsteps all spell the most sorcerish of spells
even within the shadow of her figure the devil dwells
every knock on the wood a mystery, every sound a secret
every breath is melody, but each one sinks in her regrets
and she lost the *sultan a* year ago but held her reign
over the mystic mountains and the evergreen plains
taj would break and taj would shatter
taj would get up and lose what mattered
as all empires in the past fade when they run their course
her taj would have tarnished too if it less of a glory bore
as if the glory itself is sweeping through halls of history
in late afternoons sun falls on doom but never sets us free
if you only had the privilege to see
the taj on her head of royalty
if and only you had dreamed what i had dreamed
the taj had all the glory it would have seemed
if only you had seen what i had seen
there never a better taj had been
if you were me you'd know the best
taj was held by the queen on her head
she was never ever what she seemed
she was just a light headed daydream
if beyond the royal taj you could see
she was just like you and just like me.

36. skyscrapers

it is hard to take it all seriously from this height
when everything under you is the size of nothing
and i stood there in a balcony in the sunset light
overlooking the city that goes on, soaring without wings
wealth on pleasures, smoke hangs in the air
i can't breathe in the web of the thoughts i keep
yet solitude i treasure, it's the rarest of the rare
especially in the busiest city streets
indistinct chatter of some famous affairs
i walk around on silent feet
i close my eyes and wish to be somewhere
where moon is silver and birds still sing
the city is big enough for me, that matters
all the glory, the lights and all wonderful things
great are the dreams that never let me shatter
a house is not a home and i don't intend to stay
for too long in a place and settle like dust
because higher heights in life still lay
i don't want to fall from this trust
so i move and carry on each day
for all those hopes and dreams that led me here
i have adjusted enough and donned some lies
just don't ask me how much i miss home while i'm here

because on top of the skyscrapers i longed for fireflies.

37. a gift of trust

the city of love and the one that never sleep
hear me as the thorns of midnight creep
and like roses cover the densest fields
all vows of friendship history yields
when freedom was scarce and you lived to fight
for liberty and for the age of the eternal light
you have gone down these lanes holding hands
even if there was an ocean dividing this land
they used copper for liberty as it welcomes their dreams
and iron for the tower as in moonlight it gleams
and if you wonder what keeps the iron from rust
it may be the purity of the beloved symbol of trust
a promise of friendship and a gift of love
from that height i looked at the stars above
and it's not home, not even close, but it feels like it
forever in this dream counting stars i will sit
on top of eiffel tower i remember it all of a sudden
and i remembered this tale out of the blue when
you stopped me from falling from this unhomely height
and said "if you trust the stars, why fear the light?".

38. rain clouds

i like the way it rains
and drops ease down the window pane
that i never asked for and yet
a mesmerizing pleasure it is
trickles down the glass
a thousand tiny fractals cast
mortal stains of winter dew
and the summer storm that stuck through
all washed
washed down with the water
scars on the window, gone down
all my tears washed down
back into the mud
where it came from.

summer blues.

39. lonely crowds

i walk with my head in the clouds
through lonely cities with lonely crowds
and people may fill these bustling streets
but i am lost in life, it's memory eats
festive cheers, loud music plays
no one hears what they say
and as solitary travellers tread their miles
i haven't stitched the gap it has been a while
in the middle of crowds is the loneliest place
i'd rather somewhere else with my presence grace
funny how lonely crowds can be
indifference as far as my eyes can see
though solitude is all i seek
i haven't enjoyed it, it's been some weeks
i can't see the stars in this haze
i miss the moon, it's been in a phase
running from people, stuck in crowds
unaware of the winds life brought about
so let me find solace in words
in this noise i won't go unheard
hustling for life in busy city streets
find my heart in the sky where purple and pink meet
so if you ever want to talk about the places you've seen

walking in lonely crowds is where i shall be.

40. that blue makes me sick

i woke up on a summer day, and let it be
and looked up to see the sky
it was the colour that when people see
they dream away and fantasize
so being just one of the many
i too drifted in my thoughts
of those cheery sunflower fields
a chosen memory of a lot
the sky was a sickening shade of blue
i like blue skies but not too fondly
it reminds me of all those things you do
lost in your own thoughts so lonely
the sky is blue and you liked it though
there's not a cloud, i am dying
and i feel the heat of summer woe
i like them better when they're crying
and then i stopped and dragged me out
of the warmest of my epiphany
i wonder if you still stop and think about
how the shades of sky used to be.

41. forever feels short

i held on tight to everything
to dry flowers and long lost springs
i kept my silence, i held my peace
for all i did wrong i paid the fees
and yet all that feels short
i held on to grudges, held on to pain
didn't let go of the pattering rain
i remembered all augusts and junes and mays
i remembered all the things that made my day
and yet forever feels short
i kept my joys and packed my pains
all the things that drive me insane
all the petals i wished upon
all the apples fallen in the lawn
yet forever feels short
how quickly time flies
and a memory lives and dies
and how hard i try to hold on
but what has to go will be gone
so forevers will feel short
wish upon dandelions and winds
and not upon their fragility or sins
dream upon shapes of clouds and not

upon the rain or the occasional drought

because forever never existed

dream of love and dare to fall

win it and then bare to risk it all

at last it becomes nothing and bends

beginning something means planning ends

so forevers will never be enough

so live it now and let it go

you will lose friends, make more foes

as grieves and joys in gardens tend

even bigger infinities have their ends

so forever doesn't last forever.

42. within my eyes

i have enough courage to speak
but some words still remain
unfiltered, a word they seek
swift as sun, uncertain as rain
and some words are hard to let go of
some words i simply hold through the day
my eyes may have accommodation of
just one more word i cannot say
and here each time i turn in my bed
3 a.m. at night, for my regrets
are awake long after i rest my head
my eyes can't close, echoeing words i never said
so i am just waiting for you to look into my eyes
and believe the truth it holds inside
the innocence is true and so are the cries
just look into mine before the moment dies
i don't know how it would make you feel
i don't know if you think they're lies
so i kept them concealed
each one of them within my eyes.

43. all i no more have

briefest of times
grief in the crime
fragile belief in eternity
long gone soul's serenity
unspoken but known
severity was sown
hurt without blood
fights without words
the laughter and smiles
the 'still trying' for miles
burnt the memories alive
ghosts haunt the shrine
i lived to dream
unheard screams
open air
i forget to care
counted blessing
thoughts are pressing
outnumbered by curses
the tragedy rehearses
take my hand
break this strand
the roads we left bound

crying without sound
broken trusts
hearts that rust
barely survived
lived, tried to die
summer is warm
summer is a storm
road to ruin has ended
lost what i defended.

44. the tragedy rehearses

upon a summer eve, a regal ball

to acknowledge my feelings i couldn't

and being just a miser in the hall

i fancied the tragedy i know i shouldn't

you never know when the dusk becomes dawn

worries surround me that i never think of much

maybe love was a garden of babylon

just thought of, never really touched

grace does not come easy for me

but disaster comes as character

paced across the room and tragedy

caught me walking as a disaster

so long i had danced with ghosts of my fears

only trusted wild fireflies to guide me

but then all of my fears faded with the years

no wisdom of the years could confide me

i asked my old friend tragedy of whom i knew each verse

if her treachery would make a captivating prance

and just when the tragedy began to rehearse

i asked my joy to dance.

45. cowboys

dry deserts and tumbleweeds

the heat from the burning sands

you sweat in regret of your deed

this abandoned town is where we land

you have been speaking as if i haven't heard

and you had the audacity to challenge

the one that has cactuses for words

and does not hesitate for revenge

three steps back i took

a step forward for you

but i didn't turn and you didn't look

my coldness in the eye, for you

and old fiddle lay by your feet

one with a heart around my name

too quick to judge but it seemed

the ink of love did flow in vain

to look death in the eye

or to break the head of the banjo that lay

or a solemn sacrifice

that you made for your mistakes

now that banjo was dear you are aware

maybe aware enough to let it break

but if i owned the entire world

i would have given it up for its sake
if that was a joke, i struggle to find, well,
the funny part of it amid the sand dunes
now you will never dare to smell
the sarcasm in the air of june
things break, it is still the pile of wood
tears or revenge never fix it, it is what it is
so i will just leave you to my pity as i should
you never knew love or a what a keepsake is.

46. ghost

gazing at these city lights
feeling like i'm dead inside
and i could walk through walls today
i could fly off till it's another day
when you lose what you have valued the most
you wake up in the night and haunt like a ghost
and you cry tears that vanish in the air
yet you feel too numb to even care
wander these streets with half of a soul
searching for a piece that could make me whole
and all these parties for loneliness i host
yet i pace and pace and fall like a ghost
i look at the moon i chase the sun
from heaven to hell and back i run
and then under streetlight i stand and weep
the oceans in my eyes are now a mile deep
no matter how much about my life i boast
at midnights i am always awake like a ghost
i stand and stare at how life could have been
if it were not real but only a dream
i look at the moon in my ghastly form
and i cry my tears as if a common norm
when fate comes knocking i will raise a toast

but till then i will haunt and haunt like a ghost
i look at you as in your slumber you sleep
no trace of shame on your face you keep
but a ghastly moonlit gloomy me over you
i think of the vow that was never true
fear me, pray against me to heaven and hell
till you regret me my ghost will dwell
my ghost will dwell; my ghost will dwell.

47. thoughts on a stage

can you feel it?
the heat of the spotlight that burns over my head
or is it just me?
can you feel the cold?
in the air around me where i stand
it feels like january
is my hair alright? i can't see myself...
is this moment really made of gold?
or does it only glitter
can you make sense of the chatters?
in the crowd-filled room where i stand
can they see that my nerves are about to shatter
so i'm holding my own hand
are they all looking at me and realising that i'm shaking
can they see with their shallow sight that my soul is pacing?
wish there was somewhere i could hide
the world is a stage they say, but i can't act
when i hate my character
i'm unrehearsed and that's a fact
am i trying to mould too much to fit their lies?
am i not moulding enough to be enough?
why should i mould myself when i say i'm unbreakable
i think i should conform to a form that's more feasible

deep down

wish i was invisible

no judgement, no friends, no foes

they'd never see and i'd never know.

48. matcha ice cream

the old ice cream store down the lane
my heart was full of thoughts but my words were plain
and i wanted to say and yet i was quiet
the warmth was pleasant and i held myself tight
as august ended, nothing really seemed to fall in place
confusion became a part of my resting face
and i was questioning my own existence that day
my heart was heavy and my soul was sinking
my eyes were full of dreams so i wasn't blinking
days were hard to get through and long was the night
i should learn to let go but people aren't kites
and every day i would walk to the ice cream store
to get an ice cream for joys or griefs or more
my thoughts were dissolved in the melting dream
that i saw in matcha ice cream.

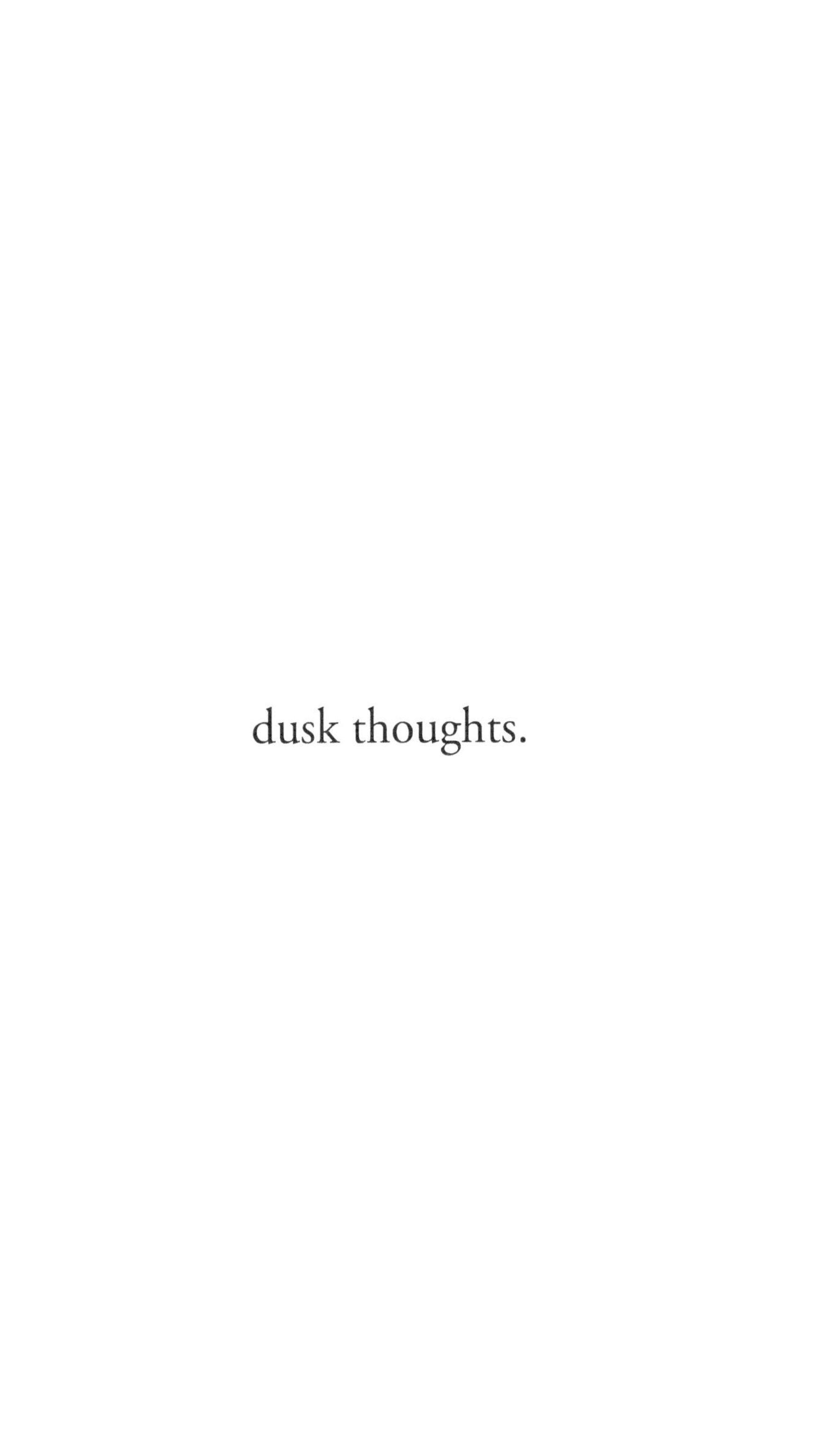

dusk thoughts.

49. weeping cosmos

when i gazed at these stars, i wondered
if i really had the strength to know
and then my silent voice thundered
i try not to but still fall for this echo
maybe my untuned strings snapped
still dead inside maybe can't even dare to try
maybe some fond memory overlapped
my experience in the years i let myself die
i was breathed back to life again but then
i let the shades of sky run my breath
when a sombre hue may tears lend
where every crimson arc delays the death
all that i have learnt about the world
and love and hope and summer dearth
and all the meaningless constellations curled
unfathomed by me, untouched by the earth
now all i do truly know about the sky
is the cosmos in dry tears is soaken
maybe that's the entire reason why
my heart looks better when it's broken.

50. watercolour

a drop of colour flows into another
and makes a mess which i worsen with a brush
and more splashed of colours roll into each other
its finally a mess that i made
more colours, more strands like watery streams
i have no control over them
it was enough to drive a control freak crazy
i have dreams but i forget to believe them
like reds and blacks splatter themselves over me
and i am afraid of ruining what i have
and my hands are stained temporarily
but i can wash it off, it's just watercolour.
i hate black and white, so monotonous and calm
i'd rather splatter colour over the most beautiful piece
i love the chaos but i don't want it to cause harm
every stroke is thought of from most to least
i swirl around the coloured water
its grey and hopeless and deprived of light
now it's all so cut and dried and i can't change it
it is in the future but it will be in the past one day
and they will all say "what mess you've made!"
trying to please everyone who comes your way and changing
colours so that they accept you as another version of you

i am afraid i will ruin the painting so i think as if it's chess
it's not artistic anymore, because chess is black and white
like a vintage film camera from the past as it spreads its light
and i run away from my past but i don't want to see the future
and what it holds
because i'm afraid they will say "you have lost all that was
yours because you couldn't be bold"
it will not be fixed because i'm not talking of watercolour
funny how it's just a metaphor of my life right now.

51. i forgot who i was

losing yourself in big cities

is like you always owned yourself on lease

and some invisible force has snatched you away

you tried to chase it but lost your way

you let go of your past and all your deeds

lost the road you came from, don't know where it leads

you can't remember when but rewind to that particular day

in my defence, i have nothing to say

the day you decided you'd never be the same

the day when you got up bruised and forgot your name

and turned into what you thought you could never become

and you became it and lost sight of the sun

you chased skyscrapers and lived for the sake of it

in the depth of futility of your search you were the hardest hit

when money never brought any more happiness than it did gold

but you couldn't free yourself from this hold

apologies if i forgot, i owe you some

here's a confession that my heart isn't truly numb

but the pain that made me different never apologised

yet i admit it was my fault that i donned a disguise

hearts of stone and lost, dead, old, innocent me

if you had ever loved me then you could still love me

feels like a piece of my heart has gone hollow

my overgrown pride is hard to swallow

if you could lead me better then i would follow

but the truth is you are just as lost as i am hollow

yet here i stand in this evening accepting all of my flaws

in the lonely crowds and lights i forgot who i was.

52. be with me

i have made mistakes, too much to ask, lord
but i still deserve to breathe in open air
and numerous chances now stain my record
and i lost each one of them
and you left
not begging for forgiveness or second chances
just a wish that wherever you go
carry a part of me, i will carry yours
remember my promises, lies and weeps
things you let go of and things you keep
remind me, i will remind you of my pains
even if as the current, run in my veins
and gentle as the snowflakes fall
remember that we had it all
and i mean well, you do too
we have problems, responsibilities too
the thin line is about to break
just promise me for destiny's sake
you were my sunsets and sunrises
this separation traumatises
the moon chases the sun to futility
my eccentric nature will learn civility
but a keepsake of all we had

remember me and i shall be glad
when you see grey and amber skies
i hope you think of my eyes
i shall carry you through life's lanes
let me live through you, all your pains
so even if as the ocean, flow through me
whatever you do just be with me
even as a bird, watch me through
the life's streams that i go to
support my sails, with me be
even if as the wind, be with me
i know i just talk never act with grace
even if as rain just fall on my face
even if as a fall upon me dawn
then enthral me like an autumn lawn
and even if i fall off my maple tree
like the wind lift me and be with me
like the tides that the mermaids brave
like the wind that washes the grave
i will let you go but you will see
forever in your memory, i will be
hope you do well and hope that you see
the beautiful world and still be with me.

53. light years in lighthouse light

it was us on a half wrecked boat

when they cast the die: it was sink or float

and we had known it long enough

the bond was strong too, if the water rough

a faint lighthouse light guided us home

i was feeling lost, but not alone

and we were dancing in the lighthouse light

we were lost but unafraid of the darkest sights

catch the wind in the sail and the moon on my face

catch the ropes and forget about all grace

all storms are destined to pass away

but not all people meant to stay

calm my hopes and quiet my fears

if death is the end then it lurks near

but the soul in my heart had a different song

the wind in my hair carried along

most can walk with me in the winds

none dare dance while it was storming

lighthouse light guide sailors to land

through perils all sailors lend each other hands

if danger is bitter by nature, this one was sweet

strangers on a limitless ocean, who may they meet?

hope on the deck where moonlight falls

take my hand, the scene enthrals

it's unrehearsed, unpredictable but at least

we were uncaring to say the least

i would not trade this life for any else

in none would i be this free of spells

i would give all to immortalise this night

i would travel fars and nears in this lighthouse light

i would travel light years in this lighthouse light.

54. holding a hell

i felt the warm air against my face
summer breeze traces its path through my soul
pity the wisdom that i don't have grace
one with the air, my heart was whole
clutching on the hot iron railings
like a memory i'm scared to lose
i told myself as if a sailor sailing
through a violent storm would do
take the moment and let it go
forget that forever existed
feel the winds and let them blow
but remember that you persisted
a memory that warms also burns you
tragedies live, moments of joy die
the flood of stories you hold inside you
no amount of words will ever signify
remember someday you will have to go
living and lying is what life is all about
even when you're gone, these winds will blow
so if you're holding a hell in you, let it out.

55. fairy in the shadows

the moment when light rain falls
and you zone out in the gentle tapping of it
on your soul
nothing more exists
you are one with the wind, water and your soul
when little drops of water softly fall on your mess of hair
and looks like a string of pearls and you no more care
about how a mess of curls catches the wind in your hair
it makes you look like a fairy in the shadows
everything disappears, insecurities and fears
your regrets and your tears and all that is
and all that isn't here
like a place in the hourglass where sands don't run
there are moments of flow like this when you go numb
to the strands of life you don't like anymore
then a wind blows and you realise it ended
it's short.
it's brief.
you have never known less grief
and you realise that you have felt more in this time
than you have in quite a while
as a fairy in the shadows
the world will never know.

56. the summer i fell from grace

a picture of grace they say
they say a dreamer of day
of day the sunflower in may
the sunflower that will wilt, they say
so a sunflower stays where it is
follows the sun down it's diurnal course
and gracefully sets its petals down
so gently with no force
that's all they want from a sunflower

but i see things differently
and the sunflower can stand tall
in the middle of rose fields
and hold heads high above them all
but that's not what they see
in the middle of perfection, they all talked
and spoke of the beauty roses bore
but the cheer in that one sunflower
tore the whole picture of grace
for grace is in being real, so let them talk

but then a sunflower rebelled and refused

how difficult life must be to hold
when all around you are perfect roses
yet you shine like your own gold
so the sunflower kept its hues
then that autumn the sunflower shed
all it's golden petals and then it's face
looked nothing like it had before
that was the summer it fell from grace
grace is in doing a little less and being a little more.

57. eternity away

the day seemed a hundred years from then
when i would forget all about it all
and live life like it was fine again
between hope and past i built a wall
and stayed by the sad side of the game
and i would never have realised
that time was flying, flying by
i couldn't stop it, dear, i wasn't wise
sunflower fields don't seem too long ago
when i had a hat on my head
and you captured it, my cheeks were red
the thought that now it was a summer ago
when i walked through the old halls
stained with old glory through all falls
in the humid july air was two summers ago
every time that i have fallen apart
now i am mended but own my scars
it was all, all so long ago
and when i thought that it would never pass
when i felt that i would be stuck in the past
and the back of my mind tainted with all the lies
these halls, these grieves, these memories will remain
then the future burst into fireflies

and the past burst into flames
and when i thought it was all just yesterday
i realised it was now an eternity away.

58. the reaper

in the middle of nowhere i stand at midnight
escaping my own shadow as it fades my light
being a ghastly form of grief i never asked for
remembering all that futility born out of war

yes, i understand we were not on the same page
but that was in the past, we needn't live in that cage
here we are and the now is what must matter
holding on to lost time, times half full in tatters

i wish i could just not listen to this hate afar
be grateful we can all peacefully see the distant stars
yes, i understand that our history is full of woe
but i don't want to stand here reaping what i did not sow.

Sunsets.

59. lifeboat

like an ocean of eyes you could drown in
strangle yourself to death in those threads
of judgement all alone and not be able to handle
those dreadful stares and the faces bare
and minds all gazing as if some expectation
from this wretched soul would save the cosmos
and that wretched soul is dazing and a haze
covers about my presence and i can't open my eyes
and the reputation lies and the spotlight blinds
and i can't dare to look myself in the eyes
and nobody else can and you are broken, in unshed tears
soaken
when all the eyes are at you including your own
including the people you would never want to let down
including the people you have let down before
and your heart has never ever felt this sore
when your reputation precedes you and your
thoughts eat you alive and you are dead inside
and you squint to find a face in the entire crowd
and even your weakest breath an echo sounds
to the point you don't want to breathe anymore
but just succumb to this web of threads of the
people you know and people you don't

and try to swim out of this flood of fear
but all against hope breakdown seems near
and then all the times you lost and will lose
if you don't stand up right now and move
and through all that shade you catch a light
from the eyes that you mostly drown in but
right now it brought you to the surface alive
had you given that look before
those first minutes wouldn't be this sore.
i would always be fine if i knew you would smile at me.

60. let a breeze take it

kept the rose
wrote the prose
burnt them both in air
daisies in a vase
heart in a case
they both wilted without a care
eyes on the road
petals in the load
dried my flowers up like this
threw the papers aside
burnt by the fireside
summer doesn't grant the wish
i had the dust of rose
half strung sad prose
broken myself can't make it
kept my heart sealed
hands on the wheel
and let a breeze take it.

61. yes, i came back

a decade old memory within my heart
of a field of corn and in my eyes a moonbeam
when the sunsets are mystic and clouds an art
when the sun shines in my eyes like a summer dream
and i, i never returned there
for all those things that kept me crowned
my reputation a thread in air
now come i homeward bound
in the air that wind was long gone
but it seemed to have left the dust
dust of memories the fields yet don
the walls had crumbled, the iron now rust
here i was again to witness the history
history within the walls of old
the legends that in the stones they bury
the stories in the book within the folds
the times that we may have long lost in time
when the sun shone silver and moon a gold
when the legends came in rhymes
the modern fates the ancient holds
so then i returned to venture in fields
to find the memory if it will redeem
and the wind was there, thy fate was sealed

i came back to see if the sunrays still hold dreams
i came back for the sunflowers and corn fields and the air
for the ecstatic vision, for the wind and the sun
for the history i never witnessed but i still care
yes i came back to see how far the shades of the sky had run.

62. conversations that will never take place

i have a confession, i talk to myself
in the lonely hours of the midnights
i contemplate the idea of heaven and hell
the mind goes on and situations i have never felt
there i stood again on the scale of justice
as it weighed every ounce of me and my sins
and the blessings and the curses and all those things
i realised i was not the only one but i was truly the one who
felt for me
yes, i plan about ages ahead because i can and i
prove to people my very worth like it's more than diamond
mines
yes, i rewind and see it in hindsight and turn back time
to all that i have faced or fought and aced
or how i should have said it better, should have burned that
letter
yes, i do live in the past trapped in a web of my own words
thinking if it was right of me or that have i even heard
but all those words, right or wrong got me here
away from their song and precipice i never cared about
yes, i think about what i have done and it was fine
yes, i have believed in myself, it was just a time

yes, i have wondered what i would say if they asked for a wish

yes, i live in my head, but that's where everything amazing is.

63. distant stars

from my window i sat and stared
dreams settling in my eyes like the midnight air
and i, looked at the distant stars
i wondered where you are
i forget often and i remind myself too
i haven't gotten used to not being around you
we miss old days and we live in the past
i would hold on forever if i could make it last
and the gold and silvers and bronzes i have gathered
but they couldn't solder my iron heart that shattered
people run their course but stars are eternal friends
i will see them every day now till the world's end
if the heavens and hells are true, i don't know where are you
but if i am ever feeling blue, the sky is where i look for you
the sunset shades look prettier back there
but you shine because the sky is yours and i'm here
if the skies ever get lonely because of distances, numb without
sound
just remember that you will always have a friend on the
ground
if the lights from other stars makes you blind
remember within you is a universe of soul you have confined
and if you feel that your heavy heart will fall off the sky

i will catch it like a shooting star and wish on it that night
the truth may keep me tied and you may not meet me soon
think you can meet me where the sun meets the moon
the worse strands of life now keep me bound
i want to show you all the people and places i have found
i want to show you the colours i put on the canvases
in the clouds, in the stories in all the unknown faces
i want to show you how far i have come
and how far along the time has run
i want to show you how i still remember
because i can never forget that december
when you sat up on your hospital bed and said you are immortal
i laughed and said the tears in my eyes were just water
but now i know i can't because you are a bit far
now i know i can't because you are in the stars.

64. nostalgia

summer camps

sunlit air

lush green grass

our feet bare

blanket forts

guarded by chair

i have problems

i forget to care

remember me

i will do the same

look at my house

when you drive this lane

cotton candy

empty stares

coloured skies

truths and dares

mystic sunsets

dreamy rose

frantic chases

by the garden hose

running scared

held you tight

in retrospect

it's black and white
stop the time
stop the world
i fantasize
autumn unfurled
kites upon
the summer breeze
emptiness that you
left in me
holiday houses
beach aside
all in dreams
i put aside
ice cream sticks
and winds that ease
magic tricks
balancing on trapeze
treehouse fun
and hammock fights
on the run
the time of our lives
that time ended
i wondered if i would ever see ya
friends for the summer
you're bittersweet nostalgia.

65. simple things

when life was easy and you spent june
lackadaisical on a couch, humming tunes
when all you knew was what you had
and had no knowledge of what you lack
when life was simple and easy for that matter
when your heart was whole, still unshattered
and all you ever wished for in the days
was a little longer summer stays
when you had never felt this blue...
i miss the simple life, don't you?

when you woke up in the day and slept at night
you still had a pretty family to hold you tight
when childish innocence was still in friends
and the mean ones were on the other side of the fence
when you didn't care what people are
you had dreams in your eyes shining like stars
when you hadn't any problems to think about
at night so you slept safe and sound
when life was summer, now it's always fall
those simple joys i had them all

when too much sweets were the greatest crime

when summer was the happiest of time
everything seems brand new to brand new eyes
but then the tainted glory of the world proves them lies
where has that little me gone? don't let her get too wise
she is lost in forest of the versions of me that i truly despise
life lay ahead but i danced around the stars
all that i knew was home, and it was never far
if i could then i would have made it last
simple things don't move so fast

when you always felt pretty no matter the hair
you loved yourself and you didn't even care
now the person that has hurt me the most
is me and my insecurities formed as ghosts
i miss all that i had, it was so good it hurts
the past had it all and now it's memory lurks
in the most grievous corners of my mind
when you saw the world not cruel but kind
damn it time, don't you tease me now
i want the simple things back, i don't know how.

66. beach

moving away is a tough job
but some moves have to be made
and you pack with you all you've got
and yet some things will still remain
like the waves that wash the shore
of this aloof town that stays here
and watches ships fare to seek the 'more'
yet all the dreamers are unaware
sandcastles and summer clouds
and yacht sails, whales and the sea
the moon and stars and voyage stories
and yet none of it can be carried with me
you can never pack a whole ocean with you
or expect to meet the sands again
and the shells that are scattered like freckles
or the smell of the salt when it rains
you can't see the sun setting in this coast
now tireless striving is what life will become
when you can no more be the holiday house host
is this the right choice or wrong, i am numb
so i will pack and leave tomorrow, that's for sure
and i can't take a part of the oceans and the sky
hence this evening, i will go to the beach for the last time

to witness the final glimpse of it with my teary eyes
i have a heart big enough to pack it all and take with me
so i may say goodbye
but i will always come back to this memory
here is where my soul shall lie.

67. koi fish pond

a blur in water the fishes swam

like a pattern of oranges and blacks

and life came gently to them

their shadows on the river bed

that gleamed with the sunlight on ripples

they were tranquil and thoughtless in their heads

under the lotus leaf they hide and seek

not seek the meaning of life, just each other

into a peaceful existence i peek

chasing each other and shadows with their angelic wings

breezing inside the cool water

that is filled by the mountain spring

i wonder what it is like to be without thoughts

and existential crises and insecurities that i keep

it's like being a koi fish in a pond of tranquillity

you float in your natural colours, in natural habitats

there's no one to say that you are too thin or too fat

when i'm stuck in this erratic current in life

i will sit here and gaze upon koi fishes

and life comes to me easily

like the wind slowed down by a forest

like the shadows of trees that hover over you, komorebi

and you drift away in this fantasy

your soul whispers "let me be!".

68. end of summer

melodramatic memories and subtle skies
it has been a while and i'm afraid it is time to say goodbye
the warm weather and mellow roses
now it's autumn and they're unfinished proses
and towards a colder air the road has bended
the summer was long but now it has ended
all the dry flowers between the story books
fantasies fade but their memory hooks
on my guitar the songs that remain unplayed
the vinyl records on which the colour aged
they've all led me here and i have defended
summer since forever but now it has ended
i hold the slipping summer between my fingers
lessons that of love there are no true harbingers
you know that summer is going to go away
when the sunsets lose their colours at the end of the day
and all the cuts that this summer gave have mended
it was rough, it was mellow but now it has ended
and there will be no sunflower fields and long lost mays
there will be no daydreams that felt like entire days
there will be no summer stars and regions
seasons will change, the world has its reasons
all the gaps are stitched and the bonds are welded

summer was beautifully harsh, but it has ended
the green leaves will dry up and they will fall
and we feel the near winter's distant call
we will chase the shade of the sky till the sun and moon
time and i will go separate ways, but we will meet soon
and to the gardens of grieves and joys i have tended
it was a good time but now this summer has ended.

I see the first leaf of autumn fall!